(*Continued at back of book*)

INCA PERU

INCA
PERU

by

C. A. BURLAND

Illustrated by

YVONNE POULTON

United States distributor
DUFOUR EDITIONS, INC.
Chester Springs, PA 19425
Tel. (215) 458-5005

HULTON EDUCATIONAL PUBLICATIONS

© 1957

ISBN 0 7175 0017 9

First published 1957
Reprinted 1962
Reprinted 1971
Reprinted 1975

HULTON EDUCATIONAL PUBLICATIONS LTD.

Raans Road, Amersham, Bucks.

Printed Offset Litho in Great Britain by
Cox & Wyman Ltd,
London, Fakenham and Reading

CONTENTS

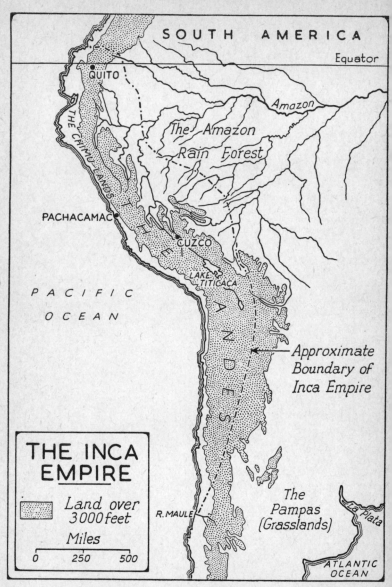

SOUTH AMERICA

Equator

QUITO

Amazon

The Amazon

Rain Forest

THE CHIMU LANDS

PACHACAMAC

CUZCO

LAKE
TITICACA

PACIFIC

OCEAN

THE ANDES

Approximate
Boundary of
Inca Empire

THE INCA
EMPIRE

Land over
3000 feet

Miles

0   250   500

R. MAULE

The
Pampas
(Grasslands)

La Plata

ATLANTIC
OCEAN

12

The Land and People

Peru is a country in South America, just south of the Equator. It lies between the Pacific Ocean and the great tropical forests of the Amazon Basin. On the coast it is very dry, almost a desert with very little rain, but the greater part of the country consists of the high table-lands and ranges of snow-capped mountains which are named the Andes. On the Pacific side it is hot and dry; beside the Amazon jungles it is hot and wet; but up on the mountain table-lands it is often quite cold, especially at night.

The people of the high-lands could grow crops of maize, potatoes and quinoa (a grain like millet), and they bred herds of the long-necked llamas. On the Pacific coasts they could grow maize, cotton, and several kinds of beans, melons and pumpkins. The Amazon forests could not be cultivated at all by the Peruvians,

Peruvian llamas

13

but the savages who lived there ate wild fruits and
cultivated a little manioc for food.

The ancient Peruvian people were American Indians
of a brownish, coppery colour. They spoke many
different languages until the Inca family came to rule
over them and made them all learn to speak the
Quechua language.

The Inca Family

For more than three thousand years people living in
Peru knew how to grow vegetables for food. They lived
in villages and towns made either of mud brick or stone.
They were a clever race, and made many fine things in
the times before the Inca family came out of the
mountains. Slowly the Incas built up their control of
the whole of the country until they ruled over an Empire
six hundred miles wide and nearly three thousand miles
long. It was so big that they called it Tahuantinsuyu,
which means The Four Quarters of the Earth.

The first Incas are said to have come to Peru from the
East. They were a family of four young people, and
they said they were the children of the Sun God. That
was only about a thousand years ago. The story tells
how they journeyed through the Andes with a wedge of

pure gold. Everywhere they stopped they put the wedge in the ground to find out if they were to stay there. At last they came to a broad valley in the heart of the country, where the wedge of gold sunk into the earth and was never seen again. Here they thought they had found the very centre of the earth. With the help of the native tribes living nearby they built a small town there which they called Cuzco.

Then, little by little, the Inca Family spread their power. For a century the descendants of the first four Incas were content to rule only the Valley of Cuzco. But attacks on them by neighbouring tribes made them realize that if they were to protect the Quechua Indians of Cuzco they must go to war. One after another the later Inca Kings fought wars to bring peace to their own people. In the reign of the twelfth Inca, the great Viracocha Inca, they had brought all the land under their rule from the Pacific Ocean to the Amazon jungle, and from the city of Quito which stands on the Equator, down south to the River Maule in Chile.

Why the Incas made an Empire

At first the Incas fought only to protect Cuzco, but later

on they decided that it would be wrong to let other tribes do as they wanted. They always feared that one day the foreign tribes might band together and destroy the Inca Empire. If that happened the Incas knew that their own people would suffer great hardships. The peaceful trade within the Empire would end. Their system of sharing food and clothing between different parts of the Empire as it was needed would break down. The temples would be destroyed, and they believed that the Sun God would not protect the people once his children, the Incas, had been driven away.

So they always worked to spread their Empire further and further. They left no important tribe in freedom; and they forced important chiefs of foreign lands to marry Inca Princesses. This was to make sure that the children of these chiefs would become relatives of the Inca, and when they grew up they would be happy to rule under the Inca Government.

The Time of Viracocha Inca

The wonderful thing about the Peruvian people in Inca times is that they made their great Empire without the help of horses, or wheeled carts, and had only the little llama to carry loads for them. There was no iron and their hardest metal was bronze. They had no real machinery, and even the splendid robes of the Inca Kings were woven on the simplest kind of hand looms. This book is written about Peru as it was in the time of the Viracocha Inca about A.D. 1450. Do not think of him as a man who lived only five hundred years ago, but as the ruler of a mighty country where wonderful things were made with none of the machines and inventions which make life so easy for us. These Peruvians of the Inca time had far less to help them than the Egyptians or Babylonians had three thousand years before them. Yet they managed to live very well and do important things like building great cities.

The City of Cuzco

The capital city of the Incas was called Cuzco. The houses were built of stone, and their roofs were made of a thick grass thatch. The important buildings were made with very big stones which had taken many men to move them into place. The streets were narrow, and often ran steeply up and down hill slopes. Only the doors and walls of the houses could be seen from the

A scene in ancient Cuzco

streets. There were no outside windows. The houses were built round open courtyards and all the windows faced inwards towards the court.

Above all other buildings, standing upon a strong platform of mighty stones was the Temple of the Sun. All round the top of this building there was a band of solid gold. The Incas believed that all gold belonged to the Sun God, so his temple was called the House of Gold. The palace of the Inca was another fine stone

18

building, but not on so high a platform as the House of the Sun. In its courtyards were store houses as well as the home of the Inca, and houses for his many wives and servants. Nearby was a convent where young ladies of good family were trained in fine embroidery and in singing for the service of the sun. In this convent they had a wonderful garden in which all the plants were made of gold and silver. But no man or boy was allowed in that house except the Inca himself.

Courtyards and storehouses of an Inca palace

In the centre of the city of Cuzco was an open space where the people met on the great festivals. On the outskirts of the city were regular rows of smaller houses where the poorer people lived. All the houses were plain, square little buildings. The doors were flat topped and on the roof was thatch four feet thick to keep out the day-time heat and the cold at night. The whole city was very orderly and neat, and it was a quiet city too with no noisy carts, but only the soft trotting of llamas and the chatter of the people going through the streets.

The Fields in the Mountains

Along the valleys outside the city and up the hillsides were maize fields. The people had made whole hillsides into terraces for growing their food. Wherever there

Terraced field on a hillside. Stone walls hold the earth in place

was earth on the slopes they took all the stones out of it to build long low walls, and then raked the earth level within the walls. In the end it looked as if the hillsides were made up of giant steps. Wherever a mountain spring burst out of the rocks they made a stone-lined channel to bring the water into the fields, and then it was led along from one field to another and not allowed to run to waste in a straight course down the hillside. One cannot count the hours and days which the Peruvian Indians spent in turning their mountain sides into fertile fields, but they did it wonderfully well, and their work has lasted until this day.

Maize Planting

The maize plant yields big cobs of good grain which make very nourishing food. To the Peruvians it was sacred. When the time came for planting maize, the very first man to dig the ground was the Inca himself. He came with the noblemen of his court to a field belonging to the Sun God, where he broke up the ground with a digging stick made of pure gold. Only the Inca could use golden tools because he was a child of the Sun. His relatives were allowed to wear golden ornaments, but no one else was allowed to keep any gold for himself.

At the maize-planting festival the Indians of every village in Peru went out into the fields. They sang hymns to the Sun and the Maize Spirit as they worked. They used a long stick about two inches wide for digging up the ground. At the end it was pointed, and often

Maize planting festival in a village

the point was fitted into a bronze blade, shaped rather like a broad chisel. A little way up the stick was a wooden footrest, and higher up a crook handle so that a man could both press and pull on his digging stick to get it into the ground more easily. When it was well in he pulled it hard towards him and so turned up the earth. Behind the row of men who were turning up the soil came a row of women with seed bags slung round their shoulders from which they spread the maize seed by handfuls. It was a happy holiday in which all the villagers worked together. In the evening they would sing, and dance to the music of their small drums and reed flutes, and drink maize beer until it was time to go to sleep.

Sharing out the Land

In Peru no one was his own master except the Inca. Everyone else was reckoned to be a part of some special group of people. They owned very little of their own. Even the land was not owned by peasant farmers. When they dug up the fields it was arranged that one field was for Inti the Sun God, one for the Inca and the third for all the people in the village. The allowance of land for the village was rationed out very exactly. There was so much for a man and so much for a woman: children and old people needed less land for their food to grow upon. As these last were not strong enough to dig up their own share of the fields the other villagers did it for them.

The Inca's share of the land was not used for the Inca and his family alone. In the Palace at Cuzco, and in every town of the great Empire of the Incas there were royal storehouses for maize and other foods. If the harvest was bad in any part of the Empire and there was not enough food for the people, the Inca sent supplies from his storehouses to help them through a difficult time. So the share of food paid to the Inca by digging

The Inca inspects his storehouses

his fields was a kind of insurance which was paid back
in time of need.

Priests and Religion

The share of land and crops belonging to the Sun God
was used for the service of the great gods of Peru, the
Rainbow, Sun and Thunder, and hundreds of other
lesser idols. The Peruvians thought there was a magic
power in everything strange and unusual. A stone with
a hole in it might bring good luck, or a great rock
naturally shaped like a puma (a wild cat sacred to their
creator god Viracocha) became a shrine where the Inca
and all his nobles made their offerings at the mid-
summer festival. Even the dried bodies of the dead were
thought to be magical and to have power to help people
who were still alive. All these things were called
"huaca" which means powerful.

In ancient Peru the priests and nuns were very
important people. In Cuzco itself there was the important House of the Ladies of the Sun where girls of noble
family and others, selected from the country villages
because of their great beauty, wove the magnificent
cloths for the temples and the gods. Not all of these

25

The Inca nobles make offerings before the sacred puma rock

girls remained nuns. If an important chief visited the Inca one of them might be given to him as his wife. But many of them remained always in the service of their gods and never married. They often became wise women who knew a great deal about healing the sick. The priests were led by the High Priest of the Sun, who was called the Villac Umu. He was nearly always a close relative of the Inca, often his brother; but other priests were chosen in many ways. Not all of them were members of the Inca family; and some of them were

26

selected from among the ordinary people of the villages because they seemed more interested in the religion than most of the people around them. The priests not only conducted the services of the gods, but they fixed the times for all festivals. They studied medicine, and also learned a lot about the minds of people so that they could give them good advice which would help them when life seemed hard and miserable.

Medicine

The ancient Peruvian medicine-men, and women, knew a great deal about illnesses and how to cure them with dieting and herbs. Often they would dance and sing over a patient and pretend to catch the spirits which had caused the illness; or they might make him believe that they worked magic to bring his lost health back again. But all this was a good thing for the simple peasant in Peru because it gave him a firm belief that he would get well again. Even today any good doctor will tell you that if you expect to get better you are on the right road to be well again. Among other things these Inca medicine men discovered were the uses of quinine to cure fevers and of cocaine to ease pain.

27

Drying and breaking up chinchona bark

They were very clever surgeons. They could put stoppings in teeth, although more often than not the stoppings were for ornament and not to cure a toothache. If a warrior was hurt in battle they knew how to set his broken bones and what herbs made the best dressings to cure his wounds. Some of them even knew how to patch a broken skull by drilling out a piece of cracked or diseased bone. We know that the patient sometimes recovered after such a serious operation, because a number of ancient Peruvian skulls show that more new bone grew around the cut after the patient

28

was well again. When the Peruvian medicine men had to do a very painful operation they made the patient drunk and then deadened pain by making him chew coca leaves, which contain cocaine. Sometimes they made him unconscious by burning special herbs under his nose.

Measuring Time

The priests measured the time of the year in ancient Peru. In every town a small observatory was attached to the Sun Temple. Here was a stone pillar called the Sun's seat (Intihuatana). The priests measured the

The Intihuatana in the Inca town of Machu Picchu

29

length of the shadow which it cast at mid-day each day. On the day when there was no shadow cast at all by the Intihuatana in the House of the Sun in Cuzco the priests knew it was the time for the great Sun Festival when the sun was directly overhead at noon. They also measured the positions on the horizon where the sun rose and set every day. Each day the positions were a little different until the next year came around. Thus they knew the date by the sun position. They were able to add to this a still more complicated calendar which they made by watching the different positions of the moon and planets every night. The priest was also the scientist in Inca Peru.

The Inca Civil Service

People gave up some of their time, food, cloth, and land for the service of the Sun and the Inca. If they did not do this the whole of Peru would have suffered. The Incas made all the arrangements for collecting this tribute through a Civil Service in which all the important jobs were done by their own relatives.

Each Inca had one Queen whose son would be the next Inca; but he had many other wives and children.

From these families came the nobles and the people who ran the Empire like a great business firm. By the time of Viracocha Inca there must have been many thousands of distant cousins of the Inca, all of whom were descended from one or other of the previous Incas. These people had the right to wear golden discs in their ears. They were the Civil Service of the Empire. Every town, big or small, had its Governor of Inca descent. In any place in the Empire one might meet some official with the golden discs in his ears. People thought that he was a man of a special kind, descended from the Sun God, so they treated him with great respect.

The String Quipus

Maybe the Inca official was a quipucamayoc, or Keeper of String Records. Such a man was very important. In his office he had a great amount of coloured string all carefully packed away in shelves. On one lot of shelves were family records of a village. They looked like bundles of coloured strings made from llama wool. When they were taken out they fell into order and looked like a long fringe of knotted strings hanging from a thick plaited cord. This cord was plaited from two or

The Keeper of String Records in his Office

three colours of string. From these colours the expert knew which village he was dealing with. The colours meant much the same to him as writing does to us. From this thick cord hung strings with knots in them. The knots were a series of round turns, like the knots on a scout's lanyard. Sometimes there was just a simple single knot, but some of the knots had eight or nine turns in them. They represented numbers, so they never had more than nine turns in them because the Incas counted as we do by tens. Each string with the knots represented the number of people in a family. If there were more than ten people in the family the first knot on the string represented the units—say three or four—and a second knot, tied a hand's breadth below represented the tens—usually one. If there had been exactly ten people there would have been no knot in the units' place and one in the tens' place.

On his main string the Keeper of String Records had a list of all the families in the village, and there were special coloured cords for the families of the Headman of Ten Families and the more important Headman of a Hundred Families.

How String Records were used

When the Keeper of the Records wanted to find out if a village had paid its dues in grain and cloth for the Storehouses of the Inca or the Temple of the Sun he would take down another set of strings. At the top the coloured cord was plaited with the same colours as the list of families. So the Keeper knew that he was dealing with the same village. But on this second cord the numbers were much bigger. They represented numbers of bags of maize and of pieces of cloth which had been paid in taxes. The numbers were tied in order of units, tens, hundreds and thousands, all marked by different positions on the coloured strings. It was just a matter of checking up the numbers of things which should have been paid in taxes against the number of people in the village.

If the account did not look right, the official with the golden earrings would send a runner up to the village.

The runner brings a message

This runner would take a message ordering the village headman to come down to make a report.

When the headman came he would sit down on the floor at the feet of the Inca official, and then they would check the accounts together. The headman would have to explain the reasons for anything wrong. His excuse must be a good one or he would be punished by a cruel beating and he would not be a headman any more. But perhaps there had been an accident such as a mountain landslide destroying some of the fields. That would have been a good reason for the shortage of goods sent in for the Inca. The official would make a note with knots on a different coloured string which he would tie on to the others. It might be that he would decide that the villagers needed a special allowance to help them out of their difficulties. Then he would send a message to the Keepers of the Storehouses of the Incas in the nearest town, and arrange for extra food and cloth to be sent up to the village.

The whole of life in Peru under the Incas was arranged by official regulations, but they were all meant to help the people of Peru. The Inca was the child of the Sun, but he felt that he was like a father to all the people who depended upon him for the good laws which made life safe and comfortable.

Village Life in the Mountains

In the little mountain villages people did not know much about the great world outside. They planted maize in their narrow strips of field on the mountain sides.

35

Further up were the hill pastures where the boys looked after herds of alpacas and llamas. The llamas were for carrying things and for meat, and the alpacas were bred for their fine wool, which was made into cloth. People kept dogs in the house to hunt the rats which tried to steal corn from the great store baskets in the house. The dog was often taken out by his master to look after the llamas. Sometimes he might have to help in a mountain hunt against some dangerous beast like a puma which killed young llamas. People would only hunt a puma if

Villagers spreading potatoes to dry in the sun

they were forced to. They thought that this big wild cat was a kind of god and they were afraid to offend it unless it turned against them.

The Peruvians were the first people to cultivate potatoes. The villagers in the high mountains grew a great many different varieties. The one they used most was called chuñu. It was a small white potato which was grown in the high plateaux. When they were dug out of the ground these small potatoes were cleaned and laid out on mats to dry and freeze in the cold mountain air. After this treatment the potatoes would keep as long as one wished. When needed for food they were ground into powder and boiled up with water into a thick potato porridge. It was very nourishing, but it had no flavour and the villagers liked to cook tasty herbs or a little meat with it.

Hunting Festivals

People went hunting on special festivals only. These were quite sacred occasions when all the people of Peru went on local hunting parties. The Inca himself joined in the local hunt near his city of Cuzco. The people made long nets and surrounded a few square miles of country, gradually closing in and catching all the deer, small animals and birds which they could find. They killed them with spears and clubs, and carried them back to the village. Most of the meat was dried and kept for future use. Among the most valued of the animals which they caught for meat was the capybara, which was like a giant guinea pig. But they kept the ordinary guinea pig, or cavy, in the house and bred it because it produced tender meat to go with their potato soup in the evenings.

Making Pottery without a Wheel

When a village happened to be near supplies of clay and sand, the women would make all their own pottery. They collected fresh clay from the rivers and carefully dried it in front of their homes. Then they powdered it and mixed fine clean sand in with the powder. When it came to be baked the sand would help the clay to take the heat without cracking. When mother wanted some pots for cooking she would wet the mixture of clay and sand until it was pliable. Then she would roll it up into balls and put them under a damp cloth in a shady corner of the hut. As the clay was wanted for use she would take one of the balls and knead it like dough until she was sure that there were no bubbles of air left in it. Then she took a little at a time and rolled it out into a long sausage shape. When she had several sausages ready she coiled them round and round, all the time pressing and turning them in her fingers until she had made them

A woman makes her household pots from coils of clay

into a single bowl with thin evenly-shaped sides. The bowl was then put into a shady corner to dry slowly. When it was nearly dry it was polished all over with a smooth pebble. This gave it a lovely shiny surface. If it was to be a very special pot mother would let it dry still more, and then paint it over very quickly with coloured clays mixed with water. Red, black, yellow and white were used. They were painted on in simple geometric designs because the people in Inca times liked that kind of pattern. After painting, the pots were again dried very carefully.

One day they were taken out for firing. The dry clay pots were piled up inside any old vase which was big enough. They liked to use a broken one through which air could flow during the firing. It was soon surrounded by a heap of dried llama dung and dry grass with a little wood added. If the wind was brisk they set light to the heap and it soon was blazing bright and hot. They kept on adding fuel all night and the old broken vase with the new pots inside it grew red hot and glowed among the flames. In the morning the fire was allowed to die down. Inside the old pot which had served as a kiln one could see the new pots slowly cooling from red hot to their natural creamy colour. While they were still very warm they were picked out with tongs made of fresh cut sticks. Then they were quickly rubbed over inside with a piece of meat fat. This filled up all the pores in the pots and made them fit to hold water.

These pots of the Inca period were always of good shapes and beautifully round and smooth although they were all modelled by the hand of the potter without any potter's wheel to help. It must have been very nice to see one's own work ready to take home for use when it had cooled down.

~~~~~~~~~~~~~~~~~~~~~~~~~~~~~~~~~~~~~~~

Markets

~~~~~~~~~~~~~~~~~~~~~~~~~~~~~~~~~~~~~~~

Of course there were a good many villages far away from clay and sand. The people who lived there had to get their pottery from the market in the nearest town. They had no money so they took down with them spare lengths of cloth, baskets, eggs, llamas, animal skins, or whatever else they had for trade. They would sit down in the town square with their goods laid out on a piece of cloth in front of them. Then people would come along and offer so much of this or that in exchange. As the market day went on they would exchange the things they had brought for pots and anything else they needed.

The markets contained all kinds of foods like tropical fruit from the coast lands, and special kinds of potato from the mountains. There were also little cloth bags filled with coca leaves. These leaves were picked off a bush which grew in the hot country. They contained a dangerous drug which made people feel content when life was hard, and gave them strength to carry heavy

A little bag for dried coca leaves

loads up the steep mountain paths when they were tired. It was dangerous because once they had started to chew coca leaves it became a habit and people could not do without it for long. It made them happy for a time but in the end it dulled their brains and made them slow and stupid. Much nicer were the sweet beans of the algarroba tree which children ate for sweets. They are sometimes called Locust Beans.

How they Dressed

When people made cloth at home, or bought it in the market it was usually for making clothes. They had no idea of tailoring clothes to fit. They wore simple straight-sided tunics made of a fold of cloth sewn up at the sides except for a space left for arm holes. A slit was made in the fold at the middle of the piece of cloth and sewn around so that one could get one's head through it. Men wore these tunics to knee length with a broad belt of brightly patterned cloth around the waist. Underneath they wore simple little breeches which were sometimes of knee length and edged with fancy coloured fringes. On the hot coastlands they wore both tunic and breeches much shorter because of the heat.

The hats worn by men were of many different kinds. Mostly they were made of a long plaited wool sling, which could be used if necessary for throwing sling stones. This was wound round and round the head like a turban and the ends tied in a fancy knot. Men from different districts wore different colours or tied the turban in different ways. On the hot coast they sometimes wore a piece of thin cloth with a string sling used just to tie it in position. One of the mountain tribes, the

Collas, wore high hats made of cane basketry. For special festivals they all loved headgear of bright coloured feathers. Among the Inca family the rank of officials was marked by a badge worn in front of their head band; it was

A man and woman in every-day dress

a little stick with a special little bunch of coloured feathers or flowers according to the position of the wearer.

Ladies dressed more simply. Their tunics were made just like those the men wore, but they were of ankle length, and they wore two or three of them of the finest cloth they could obtain. Their waistbands were broad and beautifully embroidered with bright coloured patterns. Over their shoulders they often wore a shawl which was fastened by a decorated silver pin. On their heads was a fold of white cloth worn over the forehead and hanging down the back of their neck. Men wore their hair bobbed, but the ladies combed their long black hair and wore it loose, often reaching down below their waists. Both men and women wore leather sandals, and sometimes shoes of plaited yellow grass for special occasions. They all loved jewellery and wore necklaces, earrings and bracelets.

How the Incas Prevented Revolts

It is strange but true that the Incas used the headgear of their subjects to keep them in order. They were always a little bit afraid that one or other of the local chiefs might start a revolt and break up the Empire. So they made it the law that people from each district must wear special

Inca nobles and tribal chiefs of ancient Peru

headgear. Not many of the ancient Peruvians went travelling, but if they did everyone would know where they came from by their hats.

Sometimes things went wrong in the Empire. A cruel official might make the taxes too heavy, or take too many of the young men away from a village for the army. Then the villagers might go around to other places to get other people to join them in trying to throw out the Inca Governor. Of course they would have no chance of success. Someone was sure to talk about it, and the headdress of the visitors would show where they came from. As soon as the Inca officials heard about the plot they would send their runners with the news to Cuzco. Then in a few days the Inca soldiers would come and the people of the troublesome village would be ordered to take up all their goods and march.

They would be driven from their homes and forced along the mountain roads, over the great swinging

Villagers driven across the mountains to a new homeland

bridges, up steps cut over mountain passes; and far away to another part of the Empire. Perhaps a thousand miles might be covered in such a forced journey. It would take nearly two months' walking to go that far. All the way there would be food and clothes given out by the army as the people needed them. It came from the storehouses of the Inca.

At the end of the journey they would be settled on new lands. They were now among strangers who would not join them in any plot against the Inca. But the Incas always tried to do these things as gently as possible. Instead of punishing the rebel villagers by making them pay heavier taxes and by making them do more work for the Inca it was arranged that they should pay no taxes at all for three years so that they could have time to settle down to farming in their new homeland.

The Army of the Incas

Apart from the traders with their long caravans of llamas carrying goods from one town to another, the Inca roads were mostly used by soldiers going to the wars. There was always a war in Inca Peru. Sometimes the soldiers found the war was only a kind of parade, because enemy tribes on the frontiers were often so frightened at the sight of thousands of Inca soldiers marching into their country that they gave in at once.

But sometimes there were very fierce battles around stone fortresses on the hill sides guarding the entrances to towns.

The fortress was really a group of great walls made from the biggest blocks of stone which the people of the town could roll into place. They battered them into shape with other stones until they fitted together too well to be levered apart by any attacker. Behind each wall of stones was a space filled with earth and stone chips where the defenders could run up and down to throw sling stones on the heads of the attackers or roll boulders down upon them. On the other side the attackers would use slings too, and they carried long spears with bronze points to thrust up at anyone within reach. Both sides carried clubs, which were made more deadly by a star-shaped bronze head fitted at their end. For close fighting they used a kind of bronze axe-head without a handle, with which they would chop at each other.

Soldiers wore the usual leather sandals, and the tunic belted in at the waist with a broad sash. This tunic, however, was made up of many layers of wool or cotton stitched together like a thick quilt. It could soften a heavy blow and was much lighter than metal armour would have been. The tunics of the Inca soldiers always had a bold design of coloured squares. Their heads

48

were protected by broad copper helmets, made from two sheets of copper joined at the sides, and padded inside with cloth. At the edges where the two metal sheets joined, they were decorated with fringes of coloured feathers and wool. Of course these red Indian warriors painted their faces with black, red and green. On their

A soldier of Inca Peru in war dress

arms they carried small square shields decorated with long coloured streamers which they waved as they leapt at the enemy, shouting their war cries. It must have been very brilliant and exciting to go to war in those days.

The life of the soldier was certainly not easy. There were no chariots or even carts to ease his load. Everything he needed had to be carried on his own back as he

49

marched or trotted from one place to another. If he felt overtired and hungry he would chew some coca leaves and go on in a half dream. He never worried a great deal about the hardships because he knew that all young men in Peru would serve in the army when their turn came. It was just part of growing up to them.

Besides, they all believed in their hearts that they were fighting to bring peace and happiness to other people. They were trying to save other tribes from the dangers of freedom. They knew themselves how much easier it was to serve the Inca and have everything arranged for the whole of one's life.

The army was well looked after by the Incas. Soldiers never had to take food from Peruvian homes or fields. Every few miles along the roads were storehouses of food, arms and clothing ready for use by the soldiers. It was when fighting in the country of strange tribes outside the Empire that a soldier might have to go hungry.

Those of them who came home again after the wars had a fund of strange stories to tell their friends. It was in the Inca Army that they saw the world. They marched south to the sands of the Atacama desert in Chile, or maybe they went north to bring in balsa trees from the tribal lands of Ecuador. Sometimes they would be in the mountains, sometimes they would go down to do their duty in the fortresses on the edge of the Amazon jungle, a duty which they all dreaded. But wherever they went they were seeing new places and learning new things.

~~~~~~

The Amazon Jungle and the Savages who lived there

~~~~~~

Along the edge of the mountains just above the level of the jungle the Incas built a line of small stone fortresses. There was always the danger of a raid from one or other of the savage tribes who lived in the great forest, so the fortresses were there to keep them back in their own country. But the fortresses were also places of trade. In return for maize, and cloth from Peru the Forest Indians brought fine cargoes of gorgeous macaw feathers, and monkey and jaguar skins in their canoes. But the savages could never be trusted. They swaggered about with dried heads of enemies hanging down their backs. One never knew when a quarrel with one of them might turn into an attack. But open attacks were by no means the worst danger. The savages would use bows and arrows which shot further than a Peruvian sling stone. If there was forest cover they would slip

Savages of the Amazon forests trade with Inca soldiers

from tree to tree until they were near enough to puff a dart from a blow gun at a Peruvian soldier. A scratch from such a small dart tipped with curare poison would mean death. Still worse the Inca troops always lived in fear of another invisible enemy, the fever. They knew nothing about germs, and so the fever was to them an invisible demon which could not be driven away by any magic which they knew. Because of all these things the Peruvians never attempted to conquer the scattered small tribes of the great forest. The Incas knew well enough that their soldiers could never live in this strange land of death.

The Peoples of the Pacific Coast

On the other side of the mountains the conditions were quite different. Along the desert shores of the Pacific Ocean there were peoples who had been living in towns for a great deal longer than the Incas. They were rich tribes who grew fine cotton for their clothing. They earned their food by fishing in the ocean, and by turning the short mountain rivers into ponds and canals to bring water into their fields. In this way they were able to grow enough food for all in a country where there was hardly ever any rain. They built their towns of mud brick on the edges of the deserts; and their temples and burying grounds were also in places unfit for growing food.

The most powerful people of the coast were the Chimu. At first they had a few wars with the Incas; but they were intelligent enough to realise that they could gain a lot by joining in with the Incas instead of being always at war with them. So their King married an Inca Princess and gave her more gold than she brought with her. The Chimu officials who spoke the Muchik language learnt to speak the Quechua language of the Incas, and then they all looked forward to a period of peace and happiness for their people.

Cities and Temples of the Chimu

In the Chimu cities there were fine houses all built of mud brick. Decorations on the walls of the houses were carved into the brick and painted in bright colours. The streets must have seemed to have been lined with bright coloured tapestries. There were courtyards within the bigger houses, and some of these had a small pond in them with green plants all around.

The temples of the Chimu people were also built of mud brick, and were usually quite small rooms containing an image of a god. These god-houses were put on top of a series of immense platforms of mud brick which were built one on top of the other until they looked like step-pyramids with a little thatched house on top. All the walls of the pyramids were painted with pictures of the animals sacred to the god worshipped there. Perhaps the most famous of them all was the fish god Pachacamac whose temple was painted all over with

54

An ancient tapestry
from the Chimu people
of Peru

blue and green fish. People went on pilgrimage there
from all parts of Peru because they thought that this god
knew the future, and his priests could tell them if
their life was going to be happy or not. The chief gods
of the Chimu were quite different from those of the
Inca. They did not like the hot sun which burnt up
their rainless country, so they gave first place to the
moon whom they called Si. They made his image in the
form of a little animal with a ringed tail and a moon-
shaped silver helmet on his head. The great god whom
they worshipped in common with all the peoples of Peru

55

was the creator and Lord of the Earth. He was called Kon Tiki Viracocha, and they thought of him as a great cat-like creature living beneath the earth. Upon him grew all the plants necessary for mankind to live. Of course the Inca forced them to make offerings to the Sun as well.

The Incas were friendly towards the coast people because they were a powerful tribe and grew many things which the Incas needed, such as special kinds of

A village fe

maize and tropical fruits. They also caught fresh fish and wove fine cloth from cotton—all things which the Incas could not obtain in their mountain homeland.

Cotton and Spinning

The Chimu were very clever with their cotton. They even succeeded in growing two kinds of cotton bush one

a Peru

of which gave white cotton and the other brown. They had a wonderful knowledge of dyes and could make cotton yarn of almost any colour they wished. Most of their dyes were made from plants and roots, and they were so good that many pieces of their cloth remain to this day quite unfaded.

Every woman in Peru could spin thread. As a tiny girl she began to learn to take fibres of cotton or of llama wool and twist the first few together on a wooden spindle which was shaped something like a spinning top. She kept this top spinning around as, little by little, she

Cotton bushes, and a girl spinning thread

worked more of the fibre on to it to make the thread. The spinning twisted the fibres tightly together and made the thread firm; otherwise it would pull apart. They needed so much thread that girls and women always seemed to be busy spinning. When they walked down the streets to the market they were spinning their thread all the time. Even when they sat down to talk, their busy fingers never once stopped twisting thread on the spindles. The girls of the hot coastal towns spun cotton thread. They collected the cotton bolls from the bushes and combed out the seeds. Then they made up the fibres into bunches of cotton wool from which they pulled enough fibre to make thread as they needed it.

Weaving on a Hand Loom

When they had made enough thread they wove it into cloth on a simple hand loom. There was no fine machinery to do the spinning and weaving for the ancient Peruvians; everything had to be made by hand.

First the girls took two straight sticks and placed them on pegs raised above the ground. They made sure that the distance between the pegs was just the length of the piece of cloth they wanted to make. Then they wound

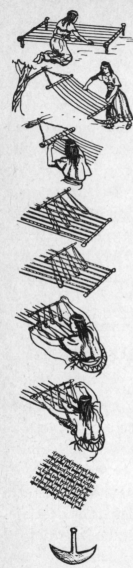

thread from one stick to another. This was the warp thread. If the cloth was going to be two yards long and two feet wide the warp would take up over a mile of thread. That was only half the thread needed to make the cloth, so you can see why the girls and women were spinning thread in every moment they had to spare.

When the warp was ready it was sewn close to the bars of wood so that it would not slip off during weaving. Next they took up the loom and tied one of the bars to a tree. The other wooden bar was tied on to a broad cloth belt which the weaver put across her back. She sat on the ground with the warp stretched in front of her. When she wanted to tighten the warp she leaned back,

Setting up a loom, and beginning to weave cloth. At the bottom is a bronze knife used by women in Peru when she wanted to loosen it she leaned forward. Next she fitted on two heddle sticks with loops of cotton so that she could pull the warp threads apart when she passed her shuttle through them. You will see from the drawings how she did it.

She went on lifting first one heddle and then the other and threading her shuttle from side to side, weaving in the weft thread which made the simple warp on the loom into a piece of cloth.

After every few rows of weaving she would pull

A woman with her tapestry loom

61

another stick towards her, which pressed all the threads close together and made the cloth firm. As the cloth grew longer she would roll it up on the loom bar nearest to her, until she had reached the other end of the loom, where it was tied to the tree. Then the cloth was finished and could be cut off the loom.

Hand loom weaving was a long and boring task but the Peruvian ladies made it more interesting by inventing bright coloured patterns to be woven into the cloth. They made many kinds of cloth, but it all had to be woven on their hand looms.

The Messengers of the Inca

The beautiful and delicate cotton cloths of the Chimu people were among the most precious tributes sent to the Inca in Cuzco. Other things which they sent were gold, silver, wood carvings, maize, black beans, red pepper, spices and even fresh fruit and fish. The fish were taken from the coast up to the mountain city of Cuzco in baskets filled with wet seaweed. The journey of about three hundred miles took only a single day. The fastest speed in ancient Peru was the pace that a man could run. So men had to take the fresh fish to the

A runner brings fresh fish to the Inca's palace in Cuzco

Inca by running with it. They had a fine smooth road all the way. Along the road were small post houses, which were huts of brick or stone in which there was food for the runners and benches for them to rest. The first runner took his basket of fish and sprinted to the first post house. As he came near it he shouted and another runner came out of the post house ready to take the fish. Then he in turn sprinted as fast as he could to the second post house, where another runner took it. One after another other runners took the basket and sprinted with

63

it for anything from half a mile to four miles. It was just like a relay race. Nobody ran very far but the fish travelled far and fast. Each messenger ran in a part of the country which he knew. Runners from the hot coast lands would never have been any good in the thinner air of the high cold mountains; on the other hand runners from the mountains would find the coast too hot and the air too heavy for them to run properly.

Messages were taken all over the country in the same way by runners so that the Inca and his officials always knew what was going on in every part of the Empire. These messengers carried a piece of wood or a knotted cord with them to remind them of the message, but as they met they called out the words to one another and passed the message on by word of mouth. They had no writing, so they could not carry letters. At the best they could carry records of the numbers of things by having knotted string quipus with them. But they were trained very carefully to learn messages by heart so that they could repeat them exactly as they were received and not get them mixed up.

The Inca Roads in the mountains

Under the Incas the Peruvians built many great roads.

The roads were needed so that messengers and the army could move quickly across the Empire. Traders used the roads too. They took goods from town to town on the backs of long caravans of llamas following each other in single file. Near Cuzco, and through all the

Traders with a caravan of llamas

mountain country, the roads were narrow and often winding. They ran along the edges of the steep valleys; sometimes they were cut into the sides of terrible precipices; occasionally they ran in tunnels cut through spurs of rock. When there was a steep climb the roads were cut as long staircases in the rock. How many thousands of people worked at battering these rocky roads into shape without the use of any metal except bronze has never been worked out. It was a mighty task so well done that the Inca roads remain till this day.

Some of the ravines in the Andes were over a mile deep, and where the roads had to cross them it was often impossible to make a staircase down to the bottom and then up again on the other side. In such places the ancient Peruvians made their great suspension bridges. First a man would take a strong cotton cord from one side of the ravine to the other. He had to climb down the cliffs, cross the raging little mountain river and then scale the cliffs on the other side. There other people met him, and hauled in the cotton cord which he had brought. Tied to the end of the cord was a strong rope. When the rope was pulled in they found the end was tied to an enormous cable. This cable had been made of plaited creepers and pliable twigs from trees. It was as thick as a man's leg and immensely strong. The far end was tied round a post and anchored by a pile of stones like a tower built on it. When it was stretched across the ravine the near end was tied down and weighted in the same way. Then a second cable was stretched across beside it. Between the two cables a footway was made of wooden boards. Then at each side a thinner rope was

A small bridge in the mountains

hung about a yard above the footway. This was the hand rail, and when it was in position the bridge was complete. The bridges were always kept in repair by people from the nearest villages who did the work as part of their tribute to the Inca. Such bridges might sway perilously in the storm winds of the high mountains, but they very rarely broke down. By inventing them the Peruvian Indians found a way of taking their roads through the almost impossible difficulties of the deep ravines and canyons of the Andes.

67

When crossing such a bridge one always looked straight in front. To look down would have been terrifying. These bridges always dipped in the middle for safety. The Incas always made them like this because the mountain mist would make the cables stretch and the sun would then make them shrink. If they were too tight they would break instead of shrinking.

Travel on the Pacific Coast

The difficulties of road builders on the Pacific coast of Peru were quite different. It was easy enough to make a path along a cultivated valley or across a ford in a river, but most of the coastland was a terrible desert of sand and rock. All they could do to mark the track was to put great beams of wood along it. These were put up on each side of the road every few yards apart. Between them the stones were cleared away as far as possible so that the road was mainly of firm sand and easy to travel upon. But these roads were made for the Inca and his army and messengers. The coast people had a far better road of their own in the Pacific Ocean where they travelled freely up and down the coast in canoes or rafts of balsa wood.

Nobody knows when the people of the Peruvian coast

first went to sea. They were fishermen even before they discovered how to grow plants for food. However, in Inca times almost every person had a small boat of one kind or another. The simplest were moon-shaped canoes made out of bundles of reeds tied tightly together. They kept the broad ends of the reeds in the middle and the narrow ends tied tightly together made up the pointed bow and stern.

Balsa Rafts

The balsa wood rafts were different. They were made from the trunks of balsa trees. These logs were never dried before the raft was made. By leaving the sap in the wood the Peruvians prevented the sea water from soaking into the soft wood too much. Otherwise the raft would not float properly. The logs were whole trees with the bark and branches trimmed off. Seven or nine of them were used to make a raft. The narrow ends of the logs were cut so as to make a rising front to the raft. Then they were tied side by side rather loosely so that the whole floating platform could move with the waves. There was a cabin in the centre of the bigger rafts, and many of them carried a mast made of two poles, one

A small balsa raft ready to set out on a coastal voyage

fixed to each side of the raft and joined together at the top. On this odd mast they hung a spar which supported a square sail of matting. If the wind was too light for the sail to be used the crew would sit at the sides and drive their raft along with big wooden paddles. It was steered, without a rudder, by long boards which had one side shaved down thin, pointing towards the front of the raft. By pushing several of these boards either up or

70

FISHING

down between the timbers of the raft it could be made to turn as one wished, but rather slowly and heavily. A balsa raft could be made of great size. Some carried forty people on trading journeys along the coast with a cargo of fine cloth, pottery and silver ornaments. The Peruvians also took these great balsa rafts far out to sea. They visited the Galapagos Islands five hundred miles out in the Pacific. It is even possible that they visited the Polynesian Islands three thousand miles away from Peru in just the same way as the Kon Tiki balsa raft was sailed to the Islands by Thor Heyerdahl and his friends in 1947. But the main use of the balsa rafts was to go up and down the coast. They sailed from town to town with their loads of pottery, gold and silver, fine cloth and other things which would not spoil in the slow voyage. If there was anything in a hurry it would be carried by messengers along the sandy coast roads instead of going on the slow balsa raft.

Fishing

The fishermen used the smaller canoes of reed bundles. In a hollow in the middle the fisherman would sit with a paddle in one hand and the end of his net in the other.

71

Fishermen in their canoe made of bundles of reeds

Sometimes they went out with hook and line. But more often little fleets of canoes each with two men would go out with the nets trailing between them. Fishermen had their own customs and their own gods including Pacha-camac. He was believed to direct them to the places where the fish would be. But from their own experience they learnt a great deal about the sea, the wind and the habits of the fish.

In some places along the coast great ridges of rock ran out to sea. These were breeding grounds for thousands

72

of seals and sea-lions. The Peruvians hunted them for food. Usually the warriors chased them with clubs and killed them with blows on their snouts.

Among the rocks they collected many kinds of shellfish including crabs. But there was something so strange about the crab that they thought it was a god and made images of it in clay with a human face on a crab's body.

Jewellery and Balances

The Peruvians were interested in shellfish for food, but they used the shells for making ornaments. They made very attractive beads in white, red, mauve or yellow shell. Some pieces of shell were cut into shapes of fish, birds, little men and monkeys. These were sewn on cotton tunics for ornament. Some of the shell pieces were set into wood or even inlaid in other shells as mosaic patterns. They were very attractive things which were traded to all parts of Peru because people liked them for their beauty.

The Chimu people in particular loved metal for jewellery. Before the Incas demanded all gold as tribute for the Sun the Chimu had worn glittering golden

Chimu silver work, and a golden spoon

earrings and necklaces. They made them in the shape of fruit and flowers. The Incas could never understand the gaiety of the Coast People; nevertheless they let them enjoy their own way of living. The Chimu were also skilled workers in silver. They made very fine vases by beating them out of a single block of silver. They would beat it out very steadily and gently until the sides were pushed up into a long thin beaker shape. These beakers were often decorated with raised patterns and faces. They were made so carefully that they had no joins either at the side or bottom.

The Chimu even tried to imitate silver in pottery.

They made their pottery from sheets of clay pressed in moulds. It was fired in the same way as the people up in the mountains fired their pots, in big old vases. But just as the burning was nearly complete the Chimu put a lot of green grass and leaves on top of the fire. That changed the colour of the pots inside to a dark grey. They were left porous and when they were filled with water the grey damp surface looked very like dull silver.

Hard stones including agate, copper carbonate, and rock crystal were cut into jewellery by polishing them into shape. They were drilled with a simple bow drill.

All this interest in jewellery made it important for the

A balance for
weighing gold

Chimu to find some way of weighing precious stones and gold and silver. They were the only people in the American Continent who invented a balance. It was quite a small thing, about as long as one's hand. From a straight beam with a loop in the middle to hold it, they hung two little cups. In one they put the precious things to be weighed, and in the other they balanced them with small stone weights. It is a curious fact that they never made a weight. They always used natural pebbles. It must have taken a lot of patience to find a natural pebble of exactly the right weight they wanted to use.

Bronze Working

The hardest metal used in Peru was bronze. They never discovered iron. The bronze was a mixture of copper and tin. They had no fixed amount of either metal in the mixture. As far as we can guess the metal workers broke up the ores and then mixed so many handfuls of each kind of crushed rock in a pottery crucible. This they put in a big fire pot filled with burning charcoal. In the sides of the pot there were many holes for the air to blow in so that it could get hotter and hotter. To help this the metal workers liked to take their pottery furnaces up to high hills where the wind blew stronger. They never invented a bellows to blow up their fires, so when the wind was not strong enough they would all sit around the furnace and blow into the holes in the sides through copper tubes. Naturally they could not melt much bronze at a time in this way. They poured it from the crucible into moulds big enough to hold a single club-head or chopper, or moon-shaped knife. If they wanted to make a bigger thing they cast a flat slab of bronze, and while it was still hot they beat it out thin into the shape they needed.

They were very clever in putting gold and silver decoration on bronze objects, and they knew how to press gold leaf on to the surface of hot bronze so as to give it a gold-plated finish.

Bronze was made into many useful things. Thin strips were beaten round and pierced to make needles. Bigger pieces were made into cloak pins and decorations for head-cloths. They used it for making pretty glittering earrings, and bells. They had bronze tweezers for pulling out hair, because they had no razors at all. They also made bronze chisels for cutting wood, and bronze points for digging sticks. A great many people in Peru found that life was made easier for them because they had bronze tools to work with.

77

Working in Stone

The stone masons who made the wonderful buildings of the Inca cities up in the mountains, found that bronze was too soft for them to work with. They had many clever ideas for making stone cutting easier, but they never invented even the simplest machine either for cutting stone or lifting blocks from one place to another.

They searched for good solid rock as near as possible to the place where they were going to build. When they found suitable stone they looked for cracks in the sheet of rock. Into these they would force wedges of dry wood. Then they would pour water over the wood to make it swell. As the wood swelled up it forced the cracks a little bit more open. Little by little this went on until after a few days the cracks had opened wide enough for a great block of stone to be broken free from its place in the mountain.

If they needed to cut a piece off the block of stone they used wood or rope dipped in wet sand and pulled to and fro like a saw. As soon as one piece was worn out they took another. It was a long task and needed much patience but they went on until the work was finished.

Next the stone had to be battered into shape until it

Breaking up a sheet of rock with wedges and water

was ready to fit into the other stones in the building which they were erecting. For this work they used balls of stone, bouncing them on the face of the building stone knocking small pieces off until it was the shape they wanted. When this was done they rolled the stone on to a number of strong wooden poles arranged like a stretcher. Two men at the ends of each pole lifted the stone. If they used enough poles they could have twenty or thirty men lifting the rough stretcher with the stone on it. Then they could walk slowly with their precious load until they could lift it into position. If the wall was high they would have a pile of earth ready, up which they could carry or push the stone into place. These big stones were very precious to them because it took so much time and hard work to make them the right shape and then to put them in place. But really big blocks of stone were only used for the foundation walls of palaces and fortresses. For smaller buildings the ancient Peru-

Shaping stones and building a stone wall

vian stone masons were wise enough to cut stones which one man could carry. They smoothed them carefully to make sure that all the joints were exactly square, so that by just laying one row of stones upon another they all balanced upright and safely one upon the other. They stayed in place because of their weight, and no mortar was used to stick them together.

The roofs of Inca period houses and palaces were simply a strong wooden framework with thick grass thatch. There were very few windows and the doors were low, so these houses were dark and gloomy in spite of the bright cloth wall hangings and the painted wooden boxes which were the only furniture. Even the Inca had no better light in his house than the flare of torches made of scented wood. But that was little worry because everybody in Peru, except the star watchers, went to bed at sunset and got up at sunrise.

Peruvian Mummies

When a Peruvian died his body was sun dried and then wrapped up in dozens of pieces of clothing, shirts, shawls, breeches and all. Some extra large cloths were wrapped round outside to make it into a tidy bundle.

On the coasts the mummy bundles were packed into graves in the sands, but in the mountains they were kept in caves or special stone houses. All around the body the relatives placed pots of food and drink to help the dead man in his journey to the land of the dead.

Offerings in memory of a dead Inca

Ordinary people were left in peace after burial. Their relatives remembered them every year and made offerings in their memory.

It was different with a dead Inca. He had been a child

of the Sun and was so mighty after his death that he was given a house and a special regiment of servants and slaves. Every year his body, beautifully dried and dressed in rich robes and feather ornaments was taken out of the cave where it was kept, and put on a splendid carrying chair. Then at a great festival it was carried into the square in Cuzco. A pure white llama was killed as a sacrifice to his spirit. Then men brought boards into the square with pictures of all the great events which had happened while this particular Inca was alive. The learned men who kept the knotted cord records then chanted the history which was painted on the boards. In this way the Peruvians learned the history of the Incas, and did honour to their memory.

How the Inca Lived

In life the Inca was still more splendid. He was served only on golden dishes. Even his sandals were made of sheets of pure gold. His clothes were specially woven by the Ladies of the Sun, and he never wore any garment a second time. After he had used it once it was either destroyed or given as a great favour to some visiting chief from another tribe. Outside the Palace the Inca was carried everywhere in a fine carrying chair with specially trained bearers. His feet rarely touched the ground except at the times of special ceremonies such as the digging of the fields in Spring. Even the great com-

The Inca and his Queen in their carrying chair

manders of the army had to crawl on all fours before him until he told them to sit on the mats at his feet. In every way he was looked upon as half a god as well as a king. Over his forehead he wore a little upright stick which bore two small blue feathers and a tuft of red wool. This was his crown, a simple little thing, but the symbol of so much power that no one else dare touch it once it had been on the head of the Inca. His word was the final law in everything. There were a number of wise old men who could advise him. But they could only stop him if he wanted to do something forbidden by some earlier Inca. Otherwise he was master of life and death. Even the High Priest was completely subject to him. His native title was Topa Inca, Only Inca, and a very true title it was.

Inca Law

The law in Peru was very strict. People believed that their Incas had made all the laws. But many of the laws were adapted by the Incas from old tribal customs which had existed long before the Inca family came to Peru. The laws were administered by Judges and officials who wore the usual big gold ear ornaments to show that they were members of the Inca family. The Judges were given their houses, clothing and food from the royal stores. They never took anything from any other Peruvian and never worked for anybody except the Inca. If they accepted a bribe the punishment was death.

Most people were careful to obey the laws. They preferred to take the easy way of sticking to the rules, and it was really very wise of them because the laws were good. But the punishments were cruel for people who broke the law. There were no prisons, so people who did wrong might have their nose or ears cut off or lose a hand, if they were not sentenced to die. Perhaps the most dreaded punishment was to be driven away from Peru to live forever more among strangers and savages.

Inca rule might be hard, but it was so wise that people hardly realised that they had lost all their freedom. They were sure of their homes and a piece of land on which to grow their food. If there was a famine the Inca fed them from his stores. If they needed clothing they had a fair share from the town storehouses, to which they had already given some of their own work. Everything was so well organised that ordinary people found nothing to worry about. Young men who had been in the army told them how different it was among the small tribes outside of Peru. The Peruvians preferred to live their own untroubled lives under the Incas, and the only stirring times they knew were their few years with the army.

~~~~~~

Schooling in Inca Peru

~~~~~~

For most boys and girls there was no regular schooling at all. But for children of Inca descent there were very strict schools. They were trained to be fit and healthy. They did a lot of running, wrestling and climbing; but also they had to know a great deal of the things we learn from books. Sometimes children of ordinary families might be sent by a chief to school in the town; but they had to be very clever, and interested in things beyond the daily work of the village. Girls were not often given schooling unless they were to be taught specially fine kinds of weaving. Inca boys and the clever lads from other families were trained to work in the Inca Civil Service. They learnt how to keep the knotted string records. They also learned a great deal about Inca laws and rules for living; and also the geography of the country. They did not learn how to read and write because there was no such thing in the country. But they were very good at arithmetic. They did their sums by counting out pebbles into little holes in the ground; and later on by making the numbers in knots on the string quipus. They had no maps of our kind for learn-

Inca boys learning arithmetic at school

ing geography, but they had models of towns and fortresses and parts of their country like relief maps. Similar models were made for architects and for the army. The Inca had models of all the towns in his Empire. Of course when a boy who had been to school went up into the army he was sure of a good position. He would know how to keep records, and also where all the Inca roads in Peru led to.

When the other children wanted to learn they had to watch their parents and the older people in the village. They soon learnt to scare birds off the growing crops

A youth with his hunting gear

and to catch animals which came into the fields in search of food. The girls learned how to spin and weave and how to make pots and to cook. The boys learned to dig the fields, to hunt and to fight. They had to make all the things for the home, like coarse mats to sleep on and wooden boxes for storing things. They made digging sticks, and braided their long slings which they wore tied round their heads until they wanted to use them. They never had time to be lazy because, with not many good tools to use they had to work much harder than we do to make anything they needed. But in between the periods of hard work the Peruvians had a good many short holidays. In particular at changes of the moon they held festivals when they made offerings to their gods, and spent much of the day in singing and dancing.

Marriages in Inca Days

One of the great festivals every year was the day when all young people of the right age were married. They did not marry just whom they liked; it was all arranged by rules. Each boy or girl could only choose from two or three people which one they would marry. When all was settled and the families had exchanged presents they waited until the Marriage Festival came. Then all the young people who were to marry that year went to the temples so that the Sun God could bless them. Then the Keepers of the Records tied the extra knots in their string quipus so that the young people would have their proper allowances of fields, seeds, and cloth. They also recorded how much work and goods the newly-married pair would have to pay as taxes. It was all very carefully arranged for them and they were happy that it was so.

When the newly-married couple returned to the

A wedding festival in the village

village everybody turned out to help them build their house. A piece of ground was cleared, and then walls of rough stones were built, held together by clay plastered in all the crevices. The roof was covered with a wooden framework tied with hide thongs. Then the thick thatch was put on. It was the longest job of all to get the thatch right; but usually such a small hut could be built very well in two days.

Later on they might have a family, but life in Inca Peru was always interesting and happy for children. They were never beaten except in school, which few of them ever saw. People thought that children should learn to be polite and kind to others, and the best way of doing that was to be kind and thoughtful when dealing with children. It was a very sensible arrangement.

The Achievements of Inca Peru

Today the Incas of Peru are mostly remembered by the stories of their wonderful treasures of gold and the tragic history of their cruel end when the Spanish Conquerors took their country in 1536. But the ancient Peruvians have many more important claims to be remembered by all of us. They discovered and used the potato, coca from which cocaine has been made, chinchona from which quinine is made. They domesticated guinea pigs and llamas and grew cotton in two colours. They built up a great empire with almost no tools or machinery to help them. They had no iron, no wheels, no horses. They made splendid roads and great suspension bridges. They discovered how to make balances for weighing things. They travelled the ocean on their simple rafts, and turned mountainsides into fields. They had no writing but kept exact records with knotted quipus and painted boards.

The secret of their success was that everything was done in an orderly way. Everybody in the Empire had something to do, and knew how and when to do it. So it all worked very well because everybody wanted it to work. That perhaps is their greatest lesson to us.